salmonpoetry

Publishing Irish & International
Poetry Since 1981

Marino Branch
Brainse Marino
Tel: 8336297

the arts council
council
an chomhairle
ealaíon

funding
literature
artscouncil.ie

An Upside Down World
KNUTE SKINNER

Marino Branch
Brainse Marino
Tel: 8336297

Published in 2019 by
Salmon Poetry
Cliffs of Moher, County Clare, Ireland
Website: www.salmonpoetry.com
Email: info@salmonpoetry.com

Copyright © Knute Skinner, 2019

ISBN 978-1-912561-76-6

All rights reserved. No part of this publication may be reproduced or transmitted in any form or by any means, electronic or mechanical, including photography, recording, or any information storage or retrieval system, without permission in writing from the publisher. The book is sold subject to the condition that it shall not, by way of trade or otherwise, be lent, resold or otherwise circulated without the publisher's prior consent in any form of binding or cover other than that in which it is published and without a similar condition, including this condition, being imposed on the subsequent purchaser.

Cover & Title Page Image:
"Unseen, Undreamt" by Sara Foust

Cover Design & Typesetting: *Siobhán Hutson*

Printed in Ireland by Sprint Print

*Salmon Poetry gratefully acknowledges the support of
The Arts Council / An Chomhairle Ealaíon*

This book is dedicated to my marriage partner

EDNA FAYE KIEL

*in gratitude for her invaluable help in editing
and proofreading the manuscript*

Contents

Angel

I heard the post drop through the slot.
It would be another of her magazines, to judge
from the thud as it hit the floor.

"Wasn't that the post?" she asked
from across the room,
adjusting the robe on her lap.

"I suppose it was," I answered,
losing my place in the *Independent*,
then running my eyes quickly
up and down the column.
I was trying to finish another story on Brexit.

Then, just as I found my place, she said,
"I know it's a bother, but would you be an angel
and put me facing the window?"

"Coming," I replied, laying the paper aside
and pushing myself from my chair.

She smiled as I turned her around
and rolled her up to the window.
"Is that where you'd like to be?" I asked.
"Are you happy here?"

"As happy as possible," she said,
raising my hand to her cheek.
"You know you make me as happy
as I'm able to be."

"That's all I can do," I answered,
slowly removing my hand,
now wet with her tears.

"I know it's a lot of bother," she continued,
"but would you be an angel and make me a cup of tea?"

"And while you're at it," she added,
as I filled the electric kettle,
"would you be an angel and see
what the post has brought us?"

The Barbecue

"I was just thinking…," I said.
"You were?" Anne questioned, and then
we both broke into laughter.

Stuart heard only our laughter,
busy as he was with his portable barbecue,
and he asked us what was so funny.

"Wally said," Anne said, "'I was just thinking…,'"
and again we broke into laughter
until Anne dropped her head on the table
and I started coughing.

"Very funny, no doubt," said Stuart
as he squirted some lighter fluid
and then reached for his matches.

"No, listen," said Anne,
straightening and gasping for air,
"you've heard only half."

The effort to speak was distorting her face,
already a deepening crimson.
"I said," she managed at last to say,
"I said to Wally, 'You were?'"

At that we began again. We laughed
until Anne blew her nose on a napkin
and I lurched over to the garden
and leaned on a birdbath.

"Oh. Very funny," said Stuart
as he lighted the charcoal.

A Bit of Cake

She placed a lump of cake on the counter,
too small for four grown men
but no doubt the best she had.
"There'll be tea in a minute," she told us
and moved to the dresser.

"No cake for me, missus," said P.J.
as she started to pull out plates.
"I'm only just after the dinner."
He moved a hand as if pushing the cake away.

"That goes the same for me," said Gus,
patting his big middle.
"I'd say I'm stretched already."

"Just some tea will be fine," said Brian.

Then they were all in chorus,
none of them able for a bite,
the three of them just after eating.
She stood by the dresser, uncertain,
the plates still in her hands.

"I'm sorry I can't offer you more," she said.
"It was good of you all to help me the way you did.
I couldn't have done it on my own."

"It was no trouble at all," P.J. answered,
and Gus and Brian said the same,
both speaking together and then repeating themselves.

"And what about you then?" she said,
her attention on me.
"Will you have some cake?"

"Well, just a bit," I replied,
as all of them looked my way.
"I shouldn't eat anything really,
but I'll take just a small cut
to go with the tea."

The Brick Path

I received Dorothy's hand,
and slowly she led me through
a long-suffering hallway
which led to a high window.
After parting the drapes,
she looked down,
and I could see what she looked at.

A brick path that threaded the lawn
was confined by tall grass, sporting thistles
and their purple blooms.
At its end a fire pit,
its stone masonry cracked,
held a black interior choked
with charred and soggy remainders.

Then, after some long-suffering minutes,
she remembered me.
"This isn't the way it used to be," she told me.
"When Laurence comes back, he must see to this.
We will have to speak to Laurence."

"Yes," I said, picking up Dorothy's hand,
"when Laurence comes back."

Marino Branch
Brainse Marino
Tel: 8336297

A Bright Morning

He stood up and kissed Mrs Warner's cheek
and then he passed through the door,
leaving behind the musky scent
of his cologne.
Footsteps sounded in the hallway.
Then the door opened and closed.

It was an intensely bright morning,
following the heavy shower,
and light poured in through the small
panes of the window.
From the next door flat came an urgent voice
as someone turned on the telly.
I took a half step closer
as if to listen.

But I heard instead the sound
of his Opel Kadett
as the engine turned over and caught.
Then Mrs Warner rose slowly to her feet,
one palm pressed flat on the table,
the other hand clutching her cotton gown
close at the throat.
Her scraggly, steel-grey hair
lay loose on her small shoulders.
"Bobby," she said, "Bobby," her voice faltering,
and she leaned hard on the table.

"There, there, Mrs Warner, it's all right,"
I said as I put my arms around her
and eased her back down.
"Sit still now and I'll put up your hair.
You want to look nice when Bobby
comes back with your doughnuts."

Carolyn and My Uncle George

I found my attention wandering,
and I looked out the window.
The lake was silver blue in the afternoon light,
and on the far bank a herd of Friesians
ranged grazing on the green slope.

"I said what do *you* think, Curtis?"
It was Mother's voice breaking in.
As I turned my eyes from the window,
I tried to hold on to an image of light
glazing the downhill side of the oak trees.

But there they sat where I'd left them,
the three graces of the manse,
my mother and my two aunts.
Sherries and ginger cakes suspended,
their eyes were focused on me.

So I coughed and reached over the table
to refill my glass.
Outside there were birds singing,
and I tried to hold on to the vision of the trees.
It was through those trees last evening
that I walked with Carolyn and Uncle George to the lake
where we listened to bird calls.

"Of what, Mother? What do you mean?" I asked,
having sipped from my sherry.
I could almost hear the stiffening of postures
in the silence that followed.

"Why, of Carolyn, of course," my mother said.
"We were talking about your uncle's new friend Carolyn."
My aunts nodded in agreement.

"Oh, Carolyn, of course, Carolyn," I said
and emptied my glass.
"I suppose she suits him well enough," I said;
"however," picking up my cue,
"I suppose if Uncle were not in such a hurry,
he might do better."

A Difficult Start

It's a difficult start—
no food, no water, no moon.
And no sense of direction.

A voice that we cannot place
floats somewhere ahead,
offering us some hope
as it flitters through shrubs and trees.

These shrubs and trees, however,
abrade our faces
as we dodge overhanging vines
and stumble on roots.

We don't know how it will end.
We only know that it is
a difficult start.

Emergent

"Everything is emergent."
That's what he said.
Emergent. I'll say that that
was a new one for me.

Then that word became the title of a poem,
and that poem became the *title* poem
of his new book:

> *Emergent and Other Poems*
> by Howard.

Just Howard—that's all the name he uses.

He does, of course, have a last name.
I found that out
when I met his father.

Howard says that if our baby is a boy,
we'll name him Howard.

And I say he's going to have
a last name as well.

"It's my baby too," I tell him.

An Escalator at Euston Station

It was a long flight of descending stairs
and, as I hastily noted,
there were two intent-looking men
positioned behind me.

I held tight to the available hand rail,
all the while knowing
there was very little that it
could do for me.

On my right side some usual ads were on view:
snack foods and West End musicals.
Nothing I needed or wanted.

But I did want to have all of them if
I did want to have them.

Am I making sense?

At the approximate halfway point
I relaxed my grip.
If they wanted to cause me maximum harm,
I said to myself,
they would surely have acted by now.

It was at this very same moment
I began to feel some pressure
behind each of my shoulders.

The Expert

I stand at the lectern, not knowing
where to begin.
They are all looking at me.
To make matters worse,
it's a muggy night in New York
and a dreadful woman has closed
the nearest window.
Perhaps if I loosen my tie.

They are all looking at me,
and I haven't much time.
I clear my throat, and then I remember,
for no good reason at all,
one spring on the Adriatic
when David, Terry and I laid siege
to the favours of Anne Louise.
A stunning blonde who served drinks
at the Bar Monique,
she moved among us with practised ease,
trading amused laughter
for our awkward proposals.
Each of us won.

But they are dead now, all dead,
and I am here as an expert
on arms control.
The woman who invited me here,
whose name eludes me,
is back on her feet again
and taking a hesitant step
in my direction.

Marino Branch
Brainse Marino
Tel: 8336297

Fawn

"That's an interesting name you have,"
he asserted.

"Fawn? It's the name they gave me," I replied.
"I would never have chosen it myself."

"Even so, it's an interesting name," he insisted,
taking one of my hands in his.
"Yours is a much more
interesting name than mine."

"I'll give it to you then," I said.
I plucked my hand from his
and held it toward him, palm up.

"There, it's yours," I told him,
"but now that you are a Fawn,
I can't expect you to go on
buying me drinks."

"Why not?" he answered, taking back my hand
and holding it close to his heart.
"You know that it's you I'm after.
It's not your name."

The Great Adventure

The taxi arrived just on time.
"Let's get going," I said to Kate
as I picked up our bag.
And then it began to rain.

We were well sprinkled by the time
we got into the taxi,
but—laughing and kissing—we were on the way
to our great adventure.

As the taxi eased onto the motorway,
Kate snuggled up against me,
and laughing, she spread her wet hair
across my face.

"Which terminal am I taking you to?"
our driver asked,
and as soon as I answered, he moved
to another lane.

At the check-in counter, we searched ourselves
and then we searched each other,
but we were not able to find
even one passport.

We ran back, laughing, to the taxi rank,
and, as if on cue, came the downpour.

A Hand on the Doorknob

I stood waiting for an answer while June
trained her eyes on a spot overhead.

As one minute slid into the next,
I advanced a step but then stopped.

The spot, whatever it was, continued
to hold her attention,
caught as she was in some spell
of self-absorption.

And then a barrage of hail
spattered the window,
and the lights, as if in response,
flickered and dimmed.

When they brightened, it was just enough
to show that nothing had changed.

"I'll go then," I said, and crossing the room,
I placed a hand on the doorknob.

A breath—just one breath—later,
June lowered her eyes.
"Where do you think you're going?" she asked.
"You'll catch your death out there."

Here and There in Sunshine

I am making slow progress toward the back wall,
fighting tall grass gone to seed
and the usual nettles, thistles and dock.
Next year, I swear, I'll get to the job sooner.

I drip with the afternoon heat,
and every surface of my body
has found some reason to itch.
When it strikes me that once again
I've forgotten the sunscreen lotion,
I take a break.

In the kitchen I drink iced tea
and look once more at the photos
that arrived in Monday's post.
Dick stands tall in the centre of Piazza San Marco,
bravely smiling and blinking away the sun.
One of the five bells, the *malefico*,
hangs as it has since 1912
when the Campanile was restored.
And I am sitting in front of our hotel,
which faces a small canal in Cannaregio,
not far from the spot where Tintoretto himself
entered the world he enhanced.

And so it goes as I plough through half the stack
and coax a few last drops from my glass.
Then I rise from the table, letting one picture slip loose
and land on the floor.
Our gondolier meets my eye as I bend over,
and his hand, as in life, is touching the brim of his hat.

In the garden I hack and yank
while muscles I didn't know I had
lodge their complaints.
I've forgotten the sunscreen again,
and I tug at my sun hat, hoping
to lengthen its shade.
Soon I will hear Dick's van coming home,
and then I can quit.

Hot Buttered Rums and the Like

The children are making snow angels
while I make myself another
hot buttered rum.
It's early in the day, but so what?
Isn't that what Christmas is for,
hot buttered rums and the like?

I can guess what my wife is doing.
She's probably still in the tub
soaking away the sick head
to which she is fully entitled.
I could take her a hair of the dog,
but she might like it better
if I washed up last night's dishes.

The tree looks surprisingly good.
She says the tinsel is cluttered,
but I do find it boring
to hang it one piece at a time.
The children are pleased with the lights
that blink on and off.

I'll be glad when this night is over.
It's a challenge putting together
those presents their mother buys them,
but then, as someone has said,
this too will pass.

And tomorrow morning will pass.
It's Christmas-on-a-Sunday this year,
and we'll have to sit through a service
with her mother and father.
There'll be dinner at their house again
and more stuff for the children.

She'll be coming down now, my one true love.
I can hear her hovering at the top of the stairs,
preparing her descent.
I'll ask her to name her poison,
and then I'll make myself another
hot buttered rum.

A Hot, Dry Day

"I'm sure you have to," she said,
and putting the tickets back in her bag,
she turned away.

"Now why did she take it that way?"
I said to no one at all
as I stood and watched her settle
into her car.
Her jumper made a bright orange contrast
to her black hair.

Then she gunned the engine,
spitting gravel behind and leaving
dust in her wake.
A squadron of starlings took flight
from the line overhead.

"I'm sure you have to, I'm sure you have to," I quoted,
stepping back and shielding my eyes
as her car grew small.
A long coil of dust diffused
and lost its shape in the dry air.

Then I turned back to my task, my heart not in it.
The sun burned hot through my shirt
as I twisted the barbed wire tight to a post
and fastened it down.
The starlings were landing on the sycamore
in Hanson's meadow.

Hot Weather

Olive had to laugh.
That's what she said later.

I had stood shifting my weight,
flowers in hand,
words just begun.

A curiously unreal sun
hung over her shaded porch
as a hot breeze lifted
strands of her hair.
Her lips pressed tight,
and then they burst open.

In days that followed, her laugh
as I redirected my steps
competed with the chugging of boats
on the sluggish river
and triumphed over the chirps
of an unknown bird.
It's a slow, hot path
from her porch to the road.

Olive didn't mean to do it,
her friend tells me,
but she just had to laugh.

House Tour

From the doorway, I hollered "Hello,"
but I heard no response.

In the hallway, I stepped through a clutter
of cast-off apparel.

The kitchen offered me only the smell
of fried fish and beer,

but upstairs I came upon Beatrice,
who lay sprawling, half dressed, on her bed.

For a piece of a minute she wiggled
her toes at me.

Then, opening her eyes, she sighed,
"Oh, it's you already."

I Go Cold with the Memory of It

I go cold with the memory of it.
If I smiled, he would smile back,
but neither of us was smiling.
It was the dead of night
in the dead centre
of a dead year.

The fire too had gone dead,
but from want of attention,
for sticks enough were at hand.
It had ceased to cast light and shadow,
but the dim bulb overhead, through flickers,
spread an indifferent aura.
A waxen pallor suffused
the lines of his face.

How long we sat there like that
I can not tell you,
but I heard a high wind come up,
and I heard it wane.

At the end, when he rose to leave,
I wanted to speak.
I wanted to break the spell, to hazard my life.
But words would not come, so instead
I reached out my hand.
He stared at my hand a moment,
then passed through the door.

An Interesting Cover

There were two wrought-iron chairs in the park—
more or less in the *middle* of the park.
I sat down on one, pretending to be absorbed
in the book I held in my hands.
I was only looking at the pages.

I was only looking at the pages,
but when a jogger paused,
just long enough to ask me about the book,
I gave it inordinate praise,
and I held it up for her view.

Yes, I gave that book inordinate praise,
although—if I speak the truth—
the book was not even mine.
I had picked it up from a bulging basket of cut-rates
in front of a nearby shop.
It *did* have an interesting cover.

Yes, it did have an interesting cover,
but the pages inside?
Well, each page looked very much
the same as another.
I opened the book to show her the title page.

And what did that woman do?
Oh, that woman waited a well-timed minute
before she sat down on the second wrought-iron chair.
She sat on the very edge of that chair
as if she was not at all certain
that that was what she should do.

I still have the book, and I still haven't read a word,
but I think—if I tried—I could write my own book
about all the minutes that followed.

In the Diner

By the time Pat showed up it was well past midnight,
and I know for a fact the concert let out at eleven,
but it's lots of fun waiting at an all-night diner—
sporting heels and a bright red dress,
drinking refills to support the coffee barons.

Oh, the streets were busy in the area all night long,
but I was witness to the only taking of life.
Why not, considering it happened outside the door—
on a pavement pale in the filtered moon—
a dozen pulsebeats beyond the big glass window.

When they came at last—Pat and his three pals—
they were laughing and high on the music and fatuously weird,
and they all took turns kissing me and spinning me around
in the fitful fluorescence of the all-night diner.
Then all they wanted to do was sit and drink coffee.

The blood on the sidewalk was not just anyone's blood—
it had swollen the cock of Pat's old high school buddy—
but Pat wouldn't have heard a word if I told him,
just coughing up stuff in a grey rag.
Besides, I wouldn't give him the satisfaction.

Kimberly

Kimberly sat down at the mirror and began
running a comb through her hair.

She uses that trick now and then
when she wants to end a discussion.

"Your hair looks all right as it is," I told her,
grabbing her chair and swivelling it toward me.
"I've got more to say to you," I added.

"Is that so?" she replied,
jabbing me in the stomach
with the point of her comb.

This happened yesterday, and today
we are going through the motions of our lives
as if nothing had happened.

They say that all's well that ends well.
That may be true, but as for me
I've yet to find out.

The Lady in the Car

"You're the lady in the car," I said,
having caught up with her on the footpath.

"And you're a damned fool,"
was her reply.

Her response disarmed me, and at first
I just watched as she strode away.
Then, recovering, I hurried after,
threading through young and old
to come up to her at a corner.

"*I'm* a damned fool?" I shouted.
"You nearly ran me over!"

She turned, fixing me with a glare.
"And you're the arsehole," she hissed
"who stepped out into the traffic."

"Now cease and desist," she added,
"before I summon a guard."

*

Cease and desist. How often
have I heard her say that?
Often enough at first, but over the years
she's been called on to say it less often.

The truth is that—over the years—
I have learned to cease and desist.

The Last Twilight

The last twilight glimmered on the water,
but we stood there clinging.
Street lights would soon be coming on behind us.
Lamps would soon be glowing
in a few of the houses along the bay—
those that were not yet boarded up
for the weather to come.
We knew we had to go back,
but we stood there clinging.

Later, a chilling breeze swept in
and bit our backs as we climbed
up the wooden steps to the promenade.
Then we scurried through empty lanes
where the last litter of the season
collected and swirled in doorways,
where the cobbles shone wet with the sweep
of a sudden downpour.

At the end, our goodbyes were brief,
late as we were,
cold and wet as we were.
Then we went our separate ways to the rentals
that housed our families for one last night.

Leftover Stew

I opened the fridge and grabbed
the nearest plastic container.
"Now what's in this one?" I asked myself
before prying open its lid.

The answer was a keen and malodorous
essence of leftover stew.

Jamming the cover back on,
I dropped the lot, both stew and container,
into the rubbish bin.

What else did I find in the fridge?
Only some other reminders
of meals well past—of meals prepared at a time
when I shared the house with someone
who cooked my dinners.

With someone, in fact, who washed and ironed
and did the shopping.
With someone who occupied half
of my king-sized bed.

"Well, things are going to change," I said,
speaking out loud to myself.
"Tomorrow I'll open one of those cookbooks.
And then I'll go to the market.
And then I'll come back here and do
a tidying up."

Having spoken my piece,
I popped open a beer
and sat down with a sigh.

And then I picked up the phone
to call out for pizza.

A Lemon Yellow

I stand here with nothing to say
and not knowing how to say it.
It has all been said before,
and none of it matters.

None of it matters.
Not to the man in charge
and not to the luckless others
who stood here before me.

The sky is a lemon yellow.
I could say that.
The grass by the stark tree
has been trodden down,

and the stark limbs
of the tree are black
against the lemon yellow
of a cloudless sky.

None of this matters at all
to the man in charge,
who, nevertheless, conforming to form,
invites me to speak.

It is my final chance.
He knows it, I know it.
And even if it matters to me,
none of it matters.

Marino Branch
Brainse Marino
Tel: 8336297

A Little Joke

Travers kept trying to kiss me,
his hands all over my blouse,
words pouring out of his mouth.

"Let me go," I said,
and I called to Bones.
As soon as Bones stood there snarling,
Travers let go.

"I didn't mean it," he said, easing off.
"It was just a joke," he added,
"a little joke between friends."
He backed away.

"I don't even want to," he blurted out,
his eyes on Bones.
That was going too far.

"Why don't you want to?" I asked him.

The sun, which threw my shadow
up to his waist, was making his eyes water.
He struggled to return my look.

"Well, of course I want to," he answered,
"but it wouldn't be fair to you.
Or fair to Billy," he added.
"It was all a joke."

"A funny joke," I said
and started to laugh.
Bending down over Bones,
I stroked his neck
and Bones stood at ease.

"Don't worry about it," I said,
rising and offering my arm.
"Billy will be in the solarium now.
Billy is a lot like Bones here.
He's always one to enjoy
a little joke between friends."

A Lovely Night

I began stacking the dishes,
but "Don't bother with those," she said,
"we can do them later."

She jumped up and crossed the room.
"Look, it's lovely out there,
with millions of stars."
She was halfway into her coat
and headed for the door.

The night was indeed lovely,
and the road that extended before us
was edged in starlight.

As we walked, the plates I had stacked
were sticking together
with grease from the chops.
The silver lay scattered on the table,
and the wine glasses and the cups
stood alone in the sink.

By this time I could have had them all
submerged in steaming hot water
and cleansing detergent.

"It's a lovely night," she said,
and she squeezed my hand.
As we neared the turn in the road,
we stopped to kiss.

Our napkins, I recalled, were ready
to be put in the laundry.

"Yes," I agreed with her,
"it's a lovely night."

A Masterful Male

He bumped into the bed
and more or less dropped me on it.
Then he stood still, taking deep breaths,
and all I could think of was the gas in my stomach
and how funny we both must look.

Then I thought of my daughter Shirley
dining somewhere by candlelight
and gazing across the table
at a hopeful smile.
Sizing it up.

Why didn't the kettle whistle?
It had gone on strike, and I lay
looking up at the pudgy gut
of my runty lover.

"It's you I want, not coffee," he said,
sitting down by my side,
acting the masterful male
but still panting a little.

Oh well, I thought, looking up
at the dust on the ceiling,
I knew we'd come here anyway
after the coffee.

The kettle had started to sing, but so what?
His stubby fingers were already
at work on my buttons.

Messy Nights

Rick signalled to the barman, pointing
to his empty glass,
but I spread my palm flat
on top of mine.
Then Rick, after paying for his drink,
gave me one of his looks.

Without a response I slipped
away to the loo,
passing through the clientele
and ignoring as best I could
some smutty glances.

Ahead of me lurked another
of our messy nights.
I'd busy myself at the hob,
and, scolding me all the while
for my glum demeanour,
he'd pour himself a skinful.

Then even as I carried our plates
over to the table,
he'd find some fault with the dinner.

Hours later, I would lie awake
reliving Rick's sour breath
and his sweaty grunts.

Midges

Midges are beginning to swarm,
and as they always do,
they find my head.

A breeze would indeed be welcome.
Or even a return of the rain
which is still dripping from the lintel
above our back window.

Through this window I can see my young bride.
An impressionist's nude,
she lies sprawling on the sheets.
Her words still swim in my head:
"Can't you put it off?"

The answer is no.
And here I am in the back garden—
waving away midges,
pushing my feet into stiff boots,
preparing to trudge a muddy field
toward what awaits me.

A Mistake

I left a message on the answering machine,
knowing it was a mistake.
Richard was in the lab already,
listening as my rapid words
were being recorded.

Or was my audience for that moment
merely the row of beakers?
Whichever, it was a mistake
to put all I had at risk.

I walked down the hall,
stopping on my way to collect
a scattering of underwear and socks.
Then dropping them into the laundry basket,
I watched through the curtains as the children's
voluptuous ball
rolled over the dewy lawn
down legions of equal grass blades.

The ball was both kicked and glittering,
both glittering and kicked.

The Moment

Julia sank back on the bed.
"It's up to you," she repeated.
It was then or never, I could see.
That was the moment.

Hovering by the door,
I looked into the hallway.
Its tedious shadows led
to lights, colours, people.

Then I took a step toward the bed,
and she covered her eyes.
"Just get it over," she muttered
and deprived me of choice.

In a moment, the moment had passed.
She rose, assembled herself,
and put on her shoes.

Laughter and chatter were spreading
in the far room.

"Let's join the party," she said.

The Morning After

The mellow morning air
brought with it the feel of autumn.
We stood at the top of the garden
appraising the roses.

One rose bush looked mildly marcesent,
but the other was a clear survivor
of the night's disturbance.
An unidentified bird loudly proclaimed
a brand-new, exuberant day.

"It's a day for starting over," I said to Paige,
reaching out and pulling her close.

"That all depends," she responded,
neither settling in nor pulling away.
"Which one of those rose bushes are we?"

My Best

Something had to be done
and sooner rather than later.

My brother Hank
offered to do it, but Hank,
as we all knew, was still
in recovery.

My sister Evelyn,
usually cocksure but never reliable,
said that whatever might happen,
she would not do it.

Shelby offered to take it on,
but that seemed too much to ask
of a summer guest.

The job was tricky enough,
but I said I would give it my best.

My best, of course,
as usual,
was not enough.

My Hands and Knees

I cleaned the floor on my hands and knees.
It was better that way.
The floor got cleaner and I didn't worry
about losing my balance.

My hands and knees are as rough as boards.
I thought once I'd soften them up
(he said I should do)
but now it's too late.

It was too late to walk to the shop.
The sky had turned black, and soon
there'd be lashings of rain.
And not in Spain either.

We were going to go there one time,
on a holiday,
but that was before he met Sammy.
A fine friend that one.

My friend Bess would be dropping by
in a couple of ticks,
so I went to the loo to do my business
and wash up a bit.

I knew we'd have to make do
with brown bread and cheese.
There wasn't a bun in the house
or a bite of sweet cake.

My Hat, a Table, and a Chair

I drop my hat on the table
and sit down on a nearby chair.
The house is quiet, but a soft light
shows under the kitchen door.
Perhaps someone is there.
Perhaps it is you.

Will I call out?—I ask myself that—
and if so, what will I say?

I locked you out of my heart—I could say that.
I locked you out of my heart
but, stubborn,
you lodged in my head.

You don't answer of course,
for I haven't spoken.
Neither have I picked up my hat
or risen from the chair.

And—if anyone is paying attention—
he or she will know
I have not taken one
step toward the kitchen.

Perhaps he or she will conclude
that I'm not really here.

My Life—Such As It Is

My life, I'll say this much at least,
has been scarred by my love
for Jocelyn Jacobi.

A car crash last year, you see,
took the life of both of her parents.
And—hard as it is to say this—
it took hers as well.

All that I have now
are a few pictures
and all of her letters.

Oh, I do also have something
I bought at an auction last week.
It's a hand-written draft
of Hershel Jacobi's first novel.

Hershel, you see, was her father.

The pages of this draft, I'm sorry to say,
are rather grubby.
And, even worse than this,
the draft is missing some pages
of the second chapter.

My Measure

Iris sealed the envelope and added a stamp.
"Here," she told me, "you can post it yourself,"
offering it to me but holding it close to her body.
"Now kiss me," she said as I moved to take it.

She accepted my kiss with a wide open, watery mouth,
then pulled me tight in her heavy arms.
The letter was still in her hand
but behind my back now.

"I have to be going, Iris," I managed at last,
but she broke away and turned to the sideboard.
"We'll have a drink first," she told me.
"Now sit down over there by the window."

"Just a small port," I answered, taking a seat
where I could see her focused face in the mirror
as well as a sloppy array of bottles.

But I bit my thumb as she started to pour.
It was easy to tell that my measure,
like all of Iris's expectations,
would be a large one.

My Story

We stood in the snow,
the tracks behind us rapidly filling in,
nothing but bright light ahead.
One direction looked
as good or as bad as another.

I thought of stories I had heard
about those who made it back
and about those who didn't.
Would I tell my own, and if not,
would anyone tell one for me?

My partner was looking my way,
awaiting decision,
confident as always that I
would come up with the answers.
The only answer that came that day
was a sickening revulsion,
a desire to rid my life
of the last seventeen years.

And now that I've done that,
I wonder how, given the chance,
I'll tell my story,
and who—if the snow ever melts—
will amend it for me.

Now What?

Henry dawdles over his coffee,
turning his cup this way and that in the saucer,
occasionally taking a sip,
then studying, as it were, its black
and lukewarm depths.
"Now what?" I wonder.

*

Henry ducks as I throw the half empty
bottles of beer.
One of them crashes into the wall behind him,
staining the paper.
One of them hits him a soft blow
on the side of the head.
"Well, what were you expecting?" I shout
as he holds his head in his hands
and begins to shudder.
Later, I kiss dry his tears,
and we end up in bed.
"It's all right," I tell him, placing
a finger on his lips.
"I'm glad that you told me."

*

Henry and I meet at a party.
He's talking to our host about stained glass when
I ask to be introduced.
His shirt and tie are a poor match.
He blinks as he tries to focus
and then favours me with a stare.
At my place, Henry is all thumbs
unlacing my boots.

On the Footpath

The footpath is empty.
I have made sure of that,
looking first to the narrow left
and then, stepping out,
to the distant right.

So far, so good.

But it's still seven tricky blocks
to my destination,
still seven intersections
to negotiate.

Not easy with the burden I bear.

The three-story townhouse I left
is now empty of life
(except for congregations
of water bugs and spiders).
Its damp-walled basement
holds all the evidence they will find.

It is just a matter of some hard minutes
to the final block,
to the place where I can sit down.

The harder problem will be
to tend to my burden.

Passing an Afternoon

The cat rose from her nap.
She took a step and stretched,
then moved away from the French door.
In the middle of the room she stopped to listen
and then looked back.
The long reach of the late afternoon sun
haloed her fur.

I returned to the book I was reading,
a birthday present.
When I found myself going back
to re-read a page,
it was time for a cup of tea.

In the kitchen I gave the cat,
who arrived there before me,
a broken-off piece of cheddar.
Then I got on with the tea
while she stretched her paw to the counter,
asking for more.

Cup in hand, I returned to the living room
and opened the book.
A selection of letters written
by a lighthouse keeper's wife,
it was not a good read.
But I kept at it, pausing only
for swallows of tea.

When at last I finished the chapter
I had promised myself,
I carried my cup to the kitchen.
The cat lay asleep by the French door
where the last rays of the sun
came filtering through.

The Patio Roses

When we slipped out into their garden
through an open window,
we decided to stay there.
What else could we have done?

Though we heard them enter the house,
there wasn't anything more
that we could do.
We would be found, with or without our bother.

The garden was small and enclosed,
mostly gravel and weeds,
but a scattering of patio roses
grew alongside one wall.

I plucked a yellow rose
to go with her blouse,
but as soon as I did so, I saw
it was all wrong.

The roses were in early bloom—
Bright Star and Little Cherub—
but the petals were already marcesent,
and the buds were beset by aphids.

Perseverance

Birds of some dirty colour
were singing at the window sill,
and I, feeling no more colourful than they,
sang along with them.

That put a stop to their noise,
and off they flew.

My eyes followed them into the air
and then onto a scrabby limb
on the aged oak.

I have to hand it to the birds.
They were soon singing again.

Pretending

Ruth pretended to be asleep, but that was okay.
That night I was willing enough
to pretend she wasn't pretending.

So I watched her a moment as she lay
with her back turned toward me,
trying to dole out slow, steady exhalations
and trying not to move as I blew soft air
on the back of her neck.

Then after a while I yawned out loud
and got out of bed,
kicking my shoe as I did so
and pretending to stumble.

Then I crossed to the window as if to look out,
not seeing a thing in the dark but just standing there
opening and closing the curtains.

Then I crossed to my dresser where I opened drawers
and then closed them again
and then slid my keys and coins
back and forth on the surface.

Through it all she lay there as still
as if she were dead,
and I spent a few minutes thinking about
what she might be thinking.
Then I walked back toward the bed,
one heavy step at a time,
and looked down at her.

One shoulder, clad in the soft light blue
of her new nighty,
was exposed where I'd pulled back the covers
as I got out of bed.
Perhaps she was feeling a chill.

I studied her shoulder and then moved
to her dressing table.
I took out the stoppers and sniffed her perfumes.
I dabbed her lotions on my neck and rubbed creams
all over my hands.
I opened her box of earrings and snapped it shut.

"Oh, I'm sorry," I said as she asked me
what I was doing,
"I'm afraid I've woken you up."

The Raspberry Tarts

We had lots of good food for Dottie's tenth birthday party.
Gertie made her renowned potato salad
while I sliced platefuls of pumpernickel, ham and cheese.
To top it all off we had pumpkin—Dottie's favourite ice cream—
as well as Gertie's raspberry tarts.

Her tarts, you could say, were as famous
as was her potato salad.
She took great pains with each tart
and always made just enough.

"Two apiece would be trouble," she always said,
and whatever she meant by that I never knew.

Well, the party did start off all right,
but then who should show up but the Koppermann twins?
Their mother had told me expressly that they couldn't make it.

But make it they did, and what could we do about it?
I offered to go without my tart, but Gertie—
well Gertie stubbornly said she would not.
(Gertie was already turning a bit funny.)

Well, in the end I asked Dottie to do without hers—
a fine thing was *that* on her birthday.

*

That party was, of course, a long time ago,
just two years before Gertie packed it all up
in a jabbering fit on the way to Emergency.

Dottie? Oh, she's away on the Florida coast.
I hear from her now and then
and always at Christmas.

She tells me she has a job working for tourists,
but I've heard rumours.

Recollection in Blue and Yellow

When I caught up, I adapted
my step to hers,
but as I did this, she turned aside.
Doing so, she stumbled and stepped
onto somebody's rain-swept lawn.

We both turned stiff, staring down
at her bright blue and yellow shoes.
They were decorated with mud.

I won't repeat what she said to me at first.
In fact, I'd as soon forget it.

It's a pleasure, however, to recall
the look that took over her face
as she stumbled over and around
some apologies and thank yous.

I didn't utter a word.
I just handed over the blue and yellow scarf
she had dropped while crossing the road.
It was not quite as muddy as her shoes.

That all happened a few years ago,
and—in case you were wondering—
we didn't fall in love or anything like that.
We didn't even have coffee.

Regrets

He went straight to his room.
That's what they say.
He went straight to his room and he shot
himself in the head.

They say he shook Sheridan's hand,
and he passed an arm through the air
in a sort of ritual blessing
on his brother's guests
(still seated at the long table).

He went straight to his room.
They could hear him ascend the stairs,
two steps at a time
(as somebody afterward put it),
and then open the door.
Their conversation had resumed
when they heard the report.

I've been told this by several of my friends.
I too was invited to the dinner,
but I had to regret.

The Reporter

From the outset, I knew,
seeing her standing there
notebook in hand,
I should keep my mouth shut.

Buying time, I deliberately
furled my umbrella,
but in time I looked up to determine
if she was still there.

What I saw were trees, sun-drenched
but offering sparkles of light
to people emerging from shop fronts
to reclaim the street.

And I recall how she looked.
A polite but amused dare
featured in her brown eyes. Her lips
were just barely drawn back.

And in spite of the dismal cast
of her sodden hair,
and in spite of the clear danger,
I found her attractive.

But I do not recall saying
the words that she said I said
when she pointed her pen at me
and repeated her question.

The Same Dog

Moments later the dog approached again,
his head bowed but his tail attempting a wag.

"That's not the same dog," said Rosie
after I pointed him out to her.
"The dog we saw earlier didn't have a tail."

"He did have a tail," I said,
"and look at it now.
That dog is trying to wag it."

Rosie made no immediate reply; she
just shrugged her shoulders.

She has magnificent shoulders,
and if you don't mind a digression,
I'll say *that* for her.
Her shoulders tan to a fine bronze,
and because of her halter top,
they were on display.

But if Rosie's shoulders were alluring,
her stance was not.
Rosie was standing tall, feet planted, glaring.

I looked past her where I could readily see
the acre or so that passes for our neighbourhood park.
Shadows cast by the trees had begun to stretch,
but a few resolute children remained
clambering onto the slides.
Everyone else had trudged away,
toting their picnic baskets.

As I turned around to pick up our own basket,
I almost stepped on the dog, and he shied away.

"The long day wanes," I said,
"so let's say we skedaddle,"
and I tossed an uneaten sandwich to the dog.

"That is not the same dog," said Rosie.

The Same Old Story

About how many hours I crawled
I can nothing say,
but the leafage on either side
grew ominously thick,
and the faithless moon no longer
shed light on the path,
and only the untoward slithering,
in the leafage on either side,
made known I was not alone.

That's how he always tells it,
and that's when, according to him,
he decided to die.
We bring him the meals which he doesn't eat—
that's according to him—
and after a while we go back
to gather up the empty plates.
It's then, if we make a mistake,
that he tells it again.

The Shopping List

I clicked the car unlocked
and swung open the door.
There, on the driver's seat, was yet
another of her shopping lists.

There was no note to me.
There was only the list.

How it came there, I don't know.
Nicole was asleep when I left our bedroom,
so she probably placed it there
before going to bed.

This time, the list was a short one:
just milk, coffee, eggs and bread
(with eggs crossed out).
It would entail just one stop
but would take me several long blocks
out of my way.

I still have that shopping list
if you'd like to see it.
Some day, when it suits my mood,
I may post it to her.

She never knew how to say *please*.

Smoke

I can see by the smoke
that he's expecting me back.
He's built up a fire in the kitchen range,
so I should feel at home.

I do feel at home, of course.
It's the life he offered me
and, small as it is, it's mine.

I won't stand here much longer,
outside our cottage door,
under this odd yellow sky,
but I know she'll be in there.

She floats in my head,
shapeless except for her child-like face
and her odd yellow hair.

She'll remain where she is…unless
he decides this is a night
for a fire in our bedroom.

I'm ready, I'm going in,
but already I can see my spirit
going up in smoke.

"So?"

"I didn't mean to do it," I said,
rising to my feet and following after
as she moved out from under the awning
and into the glare of the Tuscan sun.
"I wasn't thinking," I told her,
and I grabbed her arm.

"So?" she replied, turning toward me.
She stood, an image of contempt
such as you might encounter
in an allegorical depiction
by a Renaissance master.

She tried to free her arm,
but I held on tight and I told her again
that I didn't mean it.
In her silent response, I gave up
and let go of her arm.

Before she deigned to speak,
she brushed off her sleeve as if dirt
had landed upon it.

"Have you forgotten your old religion?" she asked.
"You should know—if anyone knows—
that you don't have to be bad
to be faced with damnation."

Someone Else

I took a seat without comment
at the end of the boat
where Ray had pointed with his finger.
He coiled up the rope a bit,
tossed it aboard,
and stepped in after.
Then he pushed off with one of the oars,
and soon we were floating freely
away from the reeds.

It was one of those close summer days,
all sunshine and little air.
The flashing sparks off the water
made my eyes sore
even after I adjusted the brim
of my floppy straw hat.
The lake was as quiet as linen
draping a corpse,
but mostly I was aware
of its sickening stench.

Someone else at my end of the boat
might have thought Ray a hero,
noting the ripple in his muscles
as he worked the oars.
Someone else might have been awed
by the mountain seemingly balanced
at the mouth of the cove
and by the indefinable
psychic union
that made up the horizon.

But that someone else,
whoever she might have been,
wasn't sitting where I was
at four o'clock in the August
of her thirtieth year,
hearing the steady rhythm
of Ray's deep breaths
and watching the steady slosh
of water at the bottom of the boat.

The Stairwell

I ran out into the street,
but there was no one to see
in either direction.

I returned to the building
and, mounting the stairs quickly,
I heard behind me their grunts.
I turned, but no one was there.
Nor was anyone on the footpath
or on the cobbles.

Back inside, I placed a foot
with care on the first step,
then turned my head.
I took another slow step,
easing up into shadows
on the dreary stairwell.
No one was there.

On the third step, I stood
with myself, with the shadows,
with an untold sequence of stairs
rising to the darkened stage
that waited for me.
I paused, holding my breath,
holding all that I knew
in precarious balance.

But then, fool that I was,
I was not content to leave
well enough alone.
Exhaling, I raised a foot
with inordinate stealth,
and when that foot pressed its claim
on a waiting stair,
I heard them again.

Stepping Out

As I stepped out her kitchen door,
I heard the lock turn behind me.
I paused briefly on the back porch,
leaning on a bare wooden railing
and taking in the view of her neighbour's garden.

A small boy was kicking and chasing a ball,
and a small dog was chasing after the boy.
I would have to pass them by
on the way to my car.

Behind me, back in the house somewhere,
was the woman with whom I'd spent the night,
the woman who had just locked the door.
To be fair, she had offered a second cup of coffee,
but she made no issue of it when I declined.

The boy stopped his kicking and chasing
when I walked past,
but the dog yapped, keen to continue their game.
When I dug a hand in my pocket,
I found that I had no car key.
It was then I remembered putting it down
on the kitchen table.

When at last the woman opened the door
to my urgent knocking,
she was holding a phone to her ear.
Moving away through the room to fetch my key,
she kept the phone where it was.
Our cups had already been washed
and placed on the drainer.

Sticky and Sweet

I went into my room and plugged in the curling iron
and the song on the radio had to remind me of Giles.

It came from the throbbing chords of a country singer
and it dripped all over with young love and early loss.
It was just the sort of song to ruin my mascara
and God knows—and all my friends it seems—
it was time for some different music.

Well the song finished and then I finished my hair
and I put on the new dress that Daddy bought me
and I found the car keys I thought I'd lost forever
and I checked out my hair and my smile in the mirror
and I set off to town for the big audition.

Well I got the part after all despite my big feet
and having to start all over a couple of times
but as I drove back through town what did I see
but a couple that could have been me and Giles
drinking coffee at a sidewalk café and both licking something
sticky and sweet from each other's fingers.

Marino Branch
Brainse Marino
Tel: 8336297

Stopped Short

"There you have it."
These words hang in the air
before drifting down on a current
and passing through a crack in the floorboards.
I watch as they disappear, and yet
I can feel them lodged in my gut.

"Is that it, then?" I say at last,
but before my words can go,
she grabs them and holds them up
as if they were wonders.
They submit to a quick perusal,
and then, with obvious contempt,
she throws them away.

I can not be sure, they are gone so soon,
that I actually spoke those words.
More words appear, however, a stream
that circles and circles my head.
"Just what were you expecting?" she says,
and then, "As usual you
expected too much."

My answer, no answer worth noting,
pursues her across the room
but is stopped short by the door
slamming it back.

A Substitute for a Dog

She cuts the meat into small pieces
and puts them a piece at a time in the dog's dish.
She has a Pomeranian, what I would call
a substitute for a dog.

Except for some dried-up food lodged
in the thick, silky hair on his chin,
he's cute, I suppose.

"Did my Snuggles enjoy his dinner?" she says,
as the last piece of meat goes down
in an unchewed swallow.

"Oh, yes," she says, in response,
"my Snuggles enjoyed his dinner."

Then, bending her ample waist, she stoops down
to gather him up to her breast.

"Isn't Snuggles the sweetest thing?" she asks,
turning toward me and presenting
the dog for inspection.

I set down my racing form, stand up,
and deposit a kiss on her powdered cheek.

"Auntie," I say, "*you're* the sweetest,"
and placing a hand on the beast,
I run my fingers over his miniature brain,
from one pointed ear to the other.

Sunshine

Sunshine streams through the overhead window,
cutting a swath of light across the cellar
and pointing my way to the wine.
I welcome its help as I find the bottle they want.
You could catch your death in that air.

Back in the kitchen, I pause for breath,
then see through parted curtains
that last night's snowfall is going fast.
The trees are already bare,
though pinpoints of coloured light
shine on their bark.
Tracks of a small animal—the neighbour's cat?—
are losing their shape in the thinning white
that layers the ground.

It's a blessing that it's going,
though the boy will be disappointed.
I can hear him already kicking the chairs.
His mother will sympathise, of course,
but his father will eye him sternly
and counsel acceptance.

And then they'll dispatch his moping face to me.
I'll have the privilege of providing
hot chocolate and scones
while they ease into their wine
and the morning papers.

That Distant Moment

The sign still read "Fasten Seat Belts"
when the captain's voice came on.
We hadn't been long in the air.

I think of that distant moment
as I pull out reliable plastic.
I think of the moments that followed
out of control.
The delirious, thrilling descent.
The total lack of a future.

I am alive, after all,
and so I remember
each minute of it.
One of the few.

For whatever reason, I'm alive,
and each ticket I buy
lessens the odds.

Marino Branch
Brainse Marino
Tel: 8336297

This Too Will Pass

When she threw her half-finished drink in his face,
he wiped his eyes.
Then he ran his tongue carefully over his lips
and turned on his heels.

"Look at him run away," she said,
glistening and gloating,
"just look at him run away."

It wasn't a welcome sight,
seeing her standing there like that,
triumphant and tarty,
and watching his shoulders grow small
as he shrank away.

I looked around me for something else
and found the surrounding faces
facing the floor.

Trees All Around

I was, I thought, the luckiest
boy in the world.
There I was in the new Buick which belonged
to the parents of Lucinda Hedley.
We were parked well down
in the woods by the lake.

I never guessed what she had in mind
when she offered to drive me home that night—
home from the Christian Youth Fellowship
at the First Presbyterian Church.

Now I'm a deacon in that same Presbyterian Church,
and the only time I'm down by the lake
is when Sally and I take the kids
for a Sunday picnic.
Sally watches them like a hawk
while I read the paper and drink a beer.
That's much to her well voiced disapproval,
but I never drink more than one.

Sally and I don't do it a lot any more,
but now and then when the kids go to bed early,
or else when they sleep over,
I can coax her into a bit of fun.
Then I close my eyes and imagine trees all around me
and can almost hear the strange sounds
that drift in off the lake.

An Upside Down World

My existence is under water
where my world mirrors another world,
the one you may see above me.

Tall trees with their rod-slim girth
stretch toward a possible sky;
but underneath these trees you will find
there are myriad reflections that embody
a many-windowed world.

There windows, with one great doorway,
give shape to my watery home.

Am I alone in this way
or does everyone live a life
of seepy reflection?

Now that is the question for an artist
to make of this liquid
semblance.

Valerie

I thought that I had shut Valerie
out of my life
but found no way to shut her out
of my memory.

She's ensconced there now.
She's inside the concert hall
the night that we find ourselves
in adjoining seats.

She's beside me the night we run stumbling,
backs hunched to a windy rain,
until we arrive at the shelter
of my dry bed.

She's slumping against a wall
dealing with tears
the night that I open my big mouth
and am rude to her mother.

And she is definitely there
on the day I push open a door
only to see her entwined
in a pair of arms.

What choice do I have now,
I ask myself,
but to entice her into
whatever new memories may come?

Walking Allison Home

"The grassy ground is already turning bare."
That's what Allison said as I walked her home.

I told her I was glad that she pointed that out.

"And the moon," she added, after a minute or so,
"hasn't it risen early?"

I disagreed with that, though somehow I
could not find the words to tell her.

But I did call her attention to a fallen tree
with a limb that extended twisty across our path.
I moved ahead and then turned to help her step over,
taking her arm gently but firmly.

She may have smiled a bit as I helped her over,
but I couldn't be sure.
My attention was mostly taken with the fallen tree
and its troublesome limb.

We advanced safely beyond that tree,
and once we had done so, Allison
extracted her arm.
She did this gently but firmly.

Then, "Isn't it cool for this time of year?" she asked me,
and I had to agree that it was.

At the end of the path, we came to an open field,
and at the other side of the field stood the house
that Allison shares with her sister.
Light was ablaze in one of the upstairs windows.

"It looks like my sister has returned home before me,"
Allison stated.
"Yes, it appears that she has,"
I said in reply.

In parting, I told her I didn't share her belief
that the moon had risen early.

Warm Colours

I sat down on the stone bench
and loosened my tie.
Marge sat serenely erect
on a wooden lawn chair,
her hands crossed neatly on one knee,
her eyes intent on some wonder
just over my shoulder.

She was wearing a cotton dress,
and her colours enhanced the glare
of the March sun.
Her tulips and hyacinths sported
a profusion of hues,
and the camillias behind them
had begun to bud.

"It's a warm day," I began,
and "It is," she answered—
in a way that acknowledged nothing
except the fine weather.

"I've come to see you …," I started,
and I paused for more words.
"I can see that," she told me.

With the merest motion she drew
her hands into her lap.

"Perhaps it's not a good time," I said,
and not thinking what I was doing,
I tightened my tie.

"Yes, it's not a good time," she replied,
"though as far as times go,
one is as good as another."

"I'll leave you then," I announced,
more sharply than I had intended.
As I stood, I loosened my tie.

"That's a nice tie," Marge said,
rising and offering her hand.
"It has warm colours."

"Like your dress," I managed to say,
and with those words
I walked out of her garden.

What I Have Assembled

The last thing I found in the trunk
was my grandfather's portrait.
Torn into bits, the pieces
lay scattered among the buttons,
the loose threads, the paper clips
and the odd mysterious scraps
on the musty bottom.

Put together, these bits formed a picture
I dimly remembered
of thick, wavy hair as black
as polished shoes,
of fierce eyebrows arched
over steely eyes,
of mutton chops sloping down
toward a starched white collar.

Who else in my life has ever
engendered awe?
Certainly not my mother, weepy and tired,
around whose misery my childhood tiptoed.
Certainly not my father, whose coarse laughter
came and went with his sudden humours
briefer than any mood.

If my sister locates me here,
her ruddy face having found me
high up in the attic, away from organisation,
will she say, "Just what are you doing now?"
Will she tell me to throw away
what I have assembled?
Will she want it herself?

What It Boils Down To

"That's what it boils down to," he said—
"fine china on the shop shelf,
the raconteur in the bar,
the bill of lading in the freight house.
You name it," he said, "and it's what
someone comes home to."

He awaited some recognition,
but I thought that his words were crazy
as I stole a last glance at his modest jaw,
the belying line of his eyebrow.
How tempting it would have been to posit
flaring nostril and flashing eye.

"That's as it may be," I told him and mounted my bike.
The road back home ran upward through narrow turns,
and soon its familiar rhythm would rise through the tyres.
"You'll see," he spat out, "you'll see—
your wife may leave you tomorrow or you may wake up
to breathe unbearable air."

What She Said

"Everything you do," said Andrea,
"has a second meaning."

It was a rare spring evening,
warm with the sound of birdsong,
fragrant with early blossom.
She wore a white low-cut blouse,
and a wispy blue cashmere shawl
lay loose on her shoulders.
That's when she said it.

From the far-off edge of the lawn
came applause and laughter as a ball
passed through a wicket.
The air was warm with the hum of approval.
"Well done," someone said.

The air where we stood was warm
with words I had uttered.
They drifted in the dwindling light.
In her hand she held the ring,
each diamond, I thought, but a paltry
reflection of love.
She lifted her eyes up to mine,
and that's when she said it.

Leabharlanna Poiblí Chathair Baile Átha Cliath
Dublin City Public Libraries

Acknowledgments

Some of these poems have previously appeared (sometimes in earlier versions) in the following periodicals and anthologies:

Agenda, Ambit Magazine, Antietam Review, The Black Mountain Review, Books Ireland, Boyne Berries, The Clare Champion, Confrontation, Crannóg, Crazyhorse, Cuírt Annual, Cyphers, Denver Quarterly, Freefall, Going Down Swinging, Grasslimb, The Hollins Critic, Hubbub, InCognito, The Kit-Kat Review, The Mid-American Review, New Ohio Review, The New York Quarterly, The New Writer, Poetry Ireland Review, Quadrant Magazine, Quantum Leap, Revival, Revival Literary Journal, The Rialto, Smiths Knoll, Snake-Nation Review, Southword, Staple, The Stony Thursday Book, Takahe, Tampa Review, Viewpoints, Vigil, Visions International, West47, Westerly, Windsor Review, and *Zed₂0.*

And some of these poems have previously appeared in a chapbook, *Against All Odds*, from Lapwing Publications, 2016.

I am grateful to The Tyrone Guthrie Centre and also to The Heinrich Böll Association for residencies during which some of these poems were written.

"Smoke" was written in response to "Smoke from Chimney, Kildimo"—an acrylic on canvas by Sara Foust.

"An Upside Down World" was written in response to "Unseen, Undreamt"—an acrylic on board by Sara Foust. This painting is part of "Flood Plain", a body of artwork on the theme of waterflow and flooding in the Inagh River valley near Ennistymon. This series explores illusions of surface and depth, reflection and disruption.

KNUTE SKINNER was born in St. Louis, Missouri, in 1929, but has had a home in Ireland since 1963. In America he has taught English and creative writing at Iowa University and at Western Washington University. Salmon Poetry has published ten previous books: nine poetry collections and a memoir. In addition, books and chapbooks of poetry have appeared from The Dolmen Press, Burton International, Northwoods Press, Aquila Press, Pierian Press, The Goliards Press, The Folly Press, Trask House Books, Pudding House Publications, Pavement Saw Press, and Lapwing Publications. A limited edition of his poems, translated into Italian by Roberto Nassi, appeared from Damocle Edizioni, Choggia, Italy. Skinner has conducted poetry workshops in Ireland and in America. He lives in Killaspuglonane, County Clare with his spouse, Edna Faye Kiel. He recently celebrated his 90th birthday.

salmonpoetry

Cliffs of Moher, County Clare, Ireland

"Like the sea-run Steelhead salmon that thrashes upstream to its spawning ground, then instead of dying, returns to the sea—Salmon Poetry Press brings precious cargo to both Ireland and America in the poetry it publishes, then carries that select work to its readership against incalculable odds."

TESS GALLAGHER

The Salmon Bookshop
& Literary Centre
Ennistymon, County Clare, Ireland